Anonymous File Sharing & Darknet - How to be a Ghost in the Machine

Lance Henderson

Table of Contents

"There is no worse tyranny than to force a man to pay for what he does not want merely because you think it should be good for him"
~ Robert Heinlein

Introduction:

At the outset, this book makes some rather simple assumptions concerning your technical knowledge. For the purposes of expediency, we'll assume that you know what an IP address is, as well as the difference between a peer-to-peer system like Emule and a torrent client like BitTorrent (not to be confused with Pirate Bay, as they are separate entities). While you certainly don't have to be a programmer, it helps to have a basic understanding of how the binary bits travel across the internet, and how various agencies monitor those bits as a means of prosecuting/persecuting those that lazily refuse to conceal their online footprint. On that topic, there is nothing extraordinarily complicated about the tools that they use to exploit the weaknesses of anonymous applications.

Most detectives as well as record industry lawyers aren't programmers either. What they use to catch downloaders and/or anti-government/environmental activists is no more complex than a carpenter using a hammer to drive a nail into a board. The training they require for using their own tools is laughably simple on the whole of it. Take your favorite photo editing application as an example. You may have used it hundreds of times, yet you are not a programmer. Would you say that using the program is obstructively difficult? Of course not. Most of the complex things take place under the hood, so to speak, as you are using it. The same is equally true of the programs law enforcement and government use to pursue tax evaders, counterfeiters, drug smugglers and the like. They hire programmers to develop a system that they can freely disperse to all agencies. Ease of use is their number one priority, as they want a program that their agents can be trained in as little time as possible. And since they have funding from the taxpayers, that means that they have a near endless supply of money with which to fine-tune and enhance said application. It is hard for private industry to compete with this, as they do not collect taxes. Profits are finite, and often unpredictable. Then there are the open-source programs that don't charge for their applications at all. They are completely reliant on donations for the further development of their tools. Examples are Truecrypt, Freenet, Tor, various incarnations of torrent clients like BitLord, BitTorrent, and the like.

It should also be stated at the outset that agencies like the NSA as well as others are constantly trying to poke holes through anonymous, onion-routing programs like Tor and Freenet, trying to discover weaknesses and exploit them, much like the hacker group Anonymous does with its seemingly endless supply of bored script kiddies. It has been argued that this actually has beneficial properties in that it provides a virtual endless supply of beta testers with which to add further enhancements and fortifications to the code. However if there is one drawback to this argument, it is that adversaries is not likely to give the developers of anonymous systems any list of exploitive bugs it found in the process. Vulnerabilities are relayed to developers by users who wish to strengthen the anonymity of the system they use, and not by those who wish to destroy it. At least, that is usually not the intention. That said, it appears that full disclosure of investigations are often relayed in court documents. This is an advantage for those who are pro-anonymity.

It doesn't always occur in such a fashion in anonymity-hostile places like Iran and China.

Chapter 1: Low-Hanging Fruit & High-Hanging Fruit: The Many and the Few

Let's perform a simple experiment and assume you live in a suburb or similarly crowded neighborhood. The weather is spectacular. People are water skiing, swimming, and even fly fishing. Now, remove all of your clothes, and then walk outside. How do you feel? Probably a bit uncomfortable. Now walk down the block with all of your valuables on full display to anyone within viewing distance. Putting aside the fact that you might be embarrassed to the core (and we'll assume no alcohol is involved), how long do you think it would be before the police arrived to pick you up, or at the very least, ask you what the hell you're doing walking nude in plain view of the public? That said, the police do not ask you such questions on p2p networks when they see something illegal going on. They setup a sting operation and try and dragnet as many people engaged in said activity as possible by casting that net far and wide long before making any public announcement to the media.

We don't want to spend too much time on the basics, but nevertheless it is needed to differentiate low hanging fruit from high hanging fruit. When you use any kind of peer-to-peer file sharing application such as Bittorrent, Emule, Limewire, Bearshare and the like, you expose your IP address to anyone on the tracker. This is a numerical value that leads straight to your doorstep. If for instance, you decide to download the latest cd by Justin Bieber (perish the thought), you can be tracked if you are not using a vpn to mask your IP address. The kicker is that you can be tracked by anyone participating in the swarm and not just law enforcement. This includes the record industry, movie industry, government agencies as well as those who connect to the system via proxified IP address.

Torrenting presents its own unique problems in that, if you are based anywhere in the US or Canada, you can be sued for millions just for downloading a few songs. How do they find you? In order to download via torrents, you have to upload simultaneously. The person on the other hand can run a netstat command (and most times this is not even required) and see your IP address. From there, the lawyer can get a judge to issue a subpoena for ISP subscriber information which has your name and address. From there, it is relatively simple to initiate all manner of lawsuits or early-dawn raids in your direction.

Peer-to-peer systems by their very design encourage sharing. Most often, users are penalized with slower download speeds if they halt of lower the speed of their uploads. This is true not only with torrents, but also p2p clients like Emule.

So how does one get around being a low hanging fruit in this manner? The answer is simple: use anonymizing tools to mask your IP address, or don't use p2p or torrents that could expose your IP address. This is not rocket science. Most p2p systems will actually let you see other IP addresses that you connect to. BitTorrent has this capability and if you have ever used it, you can even see the countries that connect to your line.

So, to summarize:

Low-Hanging Fruit = Those who persistently use peer-to-peer applications to exchange files without the use of public/private proxies, Tor, or other means of masking their identity.

High-Hanging Fruit = Those who use the Tor browser package, Freenet, I2P or similar tools to access either the web or the Freenet and I2P networks. Alternatively they can use proxies based in countries that are either hostile or have no extradition treated with the US, such as Iran, China and the like to hide their true IP location.

Identity thieves, spammers and police officers prefer to target low hanging fruit on the open web. It involves far less work, offers less risk of exposure as more tools can be used to sniff the connection, and often is the path of least resistance. It is a fact of life that most internet users will prefer the easy path to acquire or use their data/social media/finances rather than implement something that possesses a technical learning curve like Tor or Freenet.

Imagine a Chinese student who employs the use of bots on the World of Warcraft servers to mine skills/items he can later sell at some auction house. He can't make a sizeable profit doing it manually by himself, so he uses programs that do it for him. Do his bots go after the more lucrative targets which drop rare, epic weapons and armor? No, of course not. At least not initially. It is much easier to target much smaller enemies and reap the rewards of farming those kills 24/7. This is how law enforcement works. They go after the small fish, as do identity thieves, spammers and the like. Naivety and gullibility go hand in hand when you are talking about millions of users who are not too tech-savvy with their internet connections. The point of all of this is to encourage you to not be complacent in your internet habits. Don't get into the mindset of thinking that since there are millions of people out there all doing the same thing you are, that you get into a "safety in numbers" mentality.

P2P busts by law enforcement are extremely lucrative for them. When all is said and done, the government reaps profits by targeting low hanging fruit. GPS requirements for various offenders, court costs, attorney fees, asset forfeiture (i.e. taking your house if you have a grow-op present), give them millions every year, and not just for things related to P2P sharing. Record companies also reap millions in assets every year for lawsuits that usually will settle out of court for the nominal fee of about $5000 per incident of sharing mp3s. If you're one of those who absolutely insist on sharing audio online, it is highly recommended to subscribe to a premium Usenet service, as downloads are not monitored (uploads are however, but that is optional). Ten bucks a month is hardly a sacrifice when compared to a lawsuit worth tens of thousands.

"I want to be normal. I really want anonymity."
- Emma Watson

Chapter 2: Benefits of Anonymity

The term "anonymity" in and of itself can be a bit of a misnomer not only in the blogosphere but in many online forums. If the identity of a poster can be "flipped" by a forum administrator, that is, exposed, then anonymity was never a factor at all. Most likely it was privacy that a forum offered, not anonymity. And as we know, privacy and anonymity are not interchangeable terms. When you join an online forum, most of the time you are assured a fair level of privacy by the admins and moderators. That is, until you profess allegiance to Al Queda, threaten suicide or admit to committing a federal crime such as murder, etc. At that point, all bets are off, and the moderators will almost certainly give your identity to the relevant authorities voluntarily. This also applies to those in democracy-hostile countries like China, Iran and the like, where criticizing the government could land one in hot water with authorities.

As social media seeks to personalize the online social experience, the drive to expose more and more personal information about its subscribers is increasing. There seems to be the mistaken notion that if you attach your real identity to a forum post, then that post carries more "weight" in whatever argument the poster is participating. Nothing could be further from the truth. Divulging such personal info publicly:
1. Destroys any privacy OR anonymity you previously had
2. Enables ad companies like Google, Bing and Yahoo to better target your profile with laser-targeted ads not only based on your purchase history, but your religious beliefs, political persuasion and even though related family

members on social media sites like Facebook, Twitter and LinkedIn.

3. Guarantees that the information can never be satisfactorily retracted. Once it is posted on the internet, be it on forums, usenet, or blogs, it is there for the longevity of the internet.

The real question to ask is this: would you rather be engage in civil discourse with a person who reverts to ad hominem attacks and half-truths, but gives their real Facebook name and family relations, or someone who argues anonymously, but from a vantage point of logic accompanied by trusted sources that support his position? It seems that, like most democracies, we are doomed to fail if we listen to the throngs of social media users who seem to think you are more apt to be in the right if you expose your real name.

Anonymity strengthens logical arguments: Several news forums have over the past couple of years demanded its commenters to its news stories provide their real name. One such site was salemnews.com, who in 2011 took the viewpoint that using one's real name would discourage personal attacks, and encourage a more civil discourse for all readers. However a majority of their readers vehemently disagreed with that policy. I can think of one good reason it was a terrible idea: the temptation to favor influential socialites over lowly peons would definitely be too great for the editors to resist. Further, today they may demand your name. Tomorrow, you are required to not only provide your real name, but your occupation, list of coworkers, friends, and dislikes, which may include all manner of political leanings that conflict with the moderators. Once that Pandora's Box is opened, there is no closing it. Do you think FoxNews moderators are more trigger-happy with commenters who are politically left-leaning in their beliefs?

Of course they are. And the same is true with the left-leaning CNN concerning libertarian/conservative-leaning commenters. Not only can their usernames and accounts be banned, but also their IP address. This of course isn't possible if one uses the Tor network to make anonymous comments. One does not have to worry about persecution for their beliefs while using Tor. Brutal honesty it seems is on the side of anonymity, not in destroying one's personal privacy at the whims of power-hungry editors who disrespect their reader's right to privacy. Using your real identity certainly "elevates the discussion"...right into the editor's "best commenters" list. Truth is sedated by social favoritism when people in charge of our privacy overstep the boundaries that we the taxpayers paved. To make matters worse, we can already see some websites aggregating every social media link into their news comment sections. Do you really want everyone on Facebook, Twitter, Reddit and LinkedIn knowing every single thought you have on every news piece that gets delivered? How about your local politicians? Clergymen? Your Doctor?

Anonymity protects authors: Pseudonyms (pen names) protect an author's privacy like no other mechanism can. Coupled with Tor's ability to eliminate the author's true IP address, he is free to write on any subject he feels needs illumination. On the Amazon marketplace for instance, many writers employ several pen names to preserve their anonymity. Some even use Tor each and every time they access the Amazon Kindle store. It may be that they do not want their competitors knowing their true identity in order to protect the privacy of their family. Or it may be that writers of erotica do not wish their real names exposed to friends, co-workers and family members.

Anonymity protects sources: There are a multitude of examples throughout history where various sources of news were protected by anonymity. Without that anonymity, they could be prosecuted and imprisoned, or worse, retaliated against by political opponents. When an anonymous tipster wants to expose financial fraud, either involving tax funds or other illicit dealings, he does so in the faith that his trust will not be betrayed. Several hundred police websites across North America have "anonymous" tip sections of their websites. To add an extra layer to their security, users can use Tor, and rest confident in the knowledge that the police captain will not retaliate against an anonymous tipster involving his nephew who just so happens to be funneling drugs out of the station. Without the ability to use Tor, or other out-of-the-country proxies, one would inadvertently leave a trail right to their front door, all on account of their IP address that connected to the police website.

Anonymity protects free speech: In China, some use Freenet as well as Tor to send secret communiqués to each other, informing the proper news outlets of human rights abuses. However in the UK, a virtual army of surveillance cams adorn many streets with facial recognition abilities. In the US, Google CEO and social media advocate Eric Schmidt has publicly stated the difference between privacy and anonymity. Privacy in his view, was permissible. Anonymity however, was the modus operandi of terrorists, baby killers and monsters lurking in the closet. Well, maybe he wasn't quite that dramatical. However he did backpeddle when it was discovered that the Google Street car was collecting personal data on owners of wireless devices and synchronizing it with Google Maps.

In what can only be perceived as an attack on the right for an individual to use anonymous services (i.e. Tor, proxies, Freenet), he predicted the end to such tools and that law enforcement was well within its rights to do so:

"Privacy is not the same thing as anonymity. It is very important that Google and everyone else respects people's privacy. People have a right to privacy; it's natural; it's normal. It's the right way to do things. But if you are trying to commit a terrible, evil crime, it's not obvious that you should be able to do so with complete anonymity.
There are no systems in our society which allow you to do that. Judges insist on unmasking who the perpetrator was. So absolute anonymity could lead to some very difficult decisions for our governments and our society as a whole."

Apparently if you are a human rights advocate in Bejing, you're simply up to no good, according to Eric Schmidt. If you are using Tor to spread dissent, then likewise, you're up to no good. It is perhaps important to remember that Google makes far, far less money on those of us who prefer to remain anonymous. When you have javascript disabled, along with cookies, and your true IP address is concealed on Tor, it makes it near impossible for Google to track which websites you visit, log your forum comments and correlate them with your name and IP address, and build a pay-per-click profile on you. PPC is a how Google makes money: targeted advertising. It is no wonder that they do not like the idea of you hiding your shopping and commenting habits from them. When that is the case, their god-complex loses its luster.

And that folks, is what it is really about: power. They wish to strengthen the power to dictate to you what you wear, what you eat, and how you live. As an example, there is a festering phosphorescence of squabbling within the upper echelons of social media that using real names will somehow miraculously cure the ills that bullying has inflicted upon our schools. Think back to your elementary years in grade school. Most students knew who the bullies were as well as what they wore to school, what they liked and disliked and yes, what their real names were. Their bullying was not fashioned from obscurity and anonymity. Most of the bullies I encountered enacted their terrorizing publicly, albeit away from the eyes of teachers. Knowing their full names did absolutely nothing to negate their torture sessions, despite many students turning their names into the proper authorities (i.e. teachers and parents). This was back in the seventies and eighties. Back then, police officers did not trawl the school hallways looking for troublemakers. And in all honesty, has their legislated presence stopped bullying dead in its tracks? Certainly not. Then why should it if anonymity tools like Tor or Freenet are outlawed? It won't. However it would allow the powers that be even more intrusion into your life and livelihood.

The freedom to question authority is at stake. When they know everything about you, you'll be less apt to directly confront fraud when you see it, for fear of reprisal. Back in elementary school, one could always anonymously inform the principle of some wrong-doing or bully who didn't respect the human rights of others. Slip a note under an office door perhaps. With cameras and police patrolling the schools, it seems less likely now. The power given by the people to legislators, teachers and politicians has been deemed insufficient. Now they want more, and the expedition starts with places like Facebook, Google, Microsoft and LinkedIn coalescing into a conglomerate of corporate nanny-staters who want to profit on your private life. Both government and private enterprise have issued the order of full steam ahead in enacting such a bureaucratic monstrosity.

"I am not the first man who wanted to make changes in his life at 60 and I won't be the last. It is just that others can do it with anonymity."
- Harrison Ford

Chapter 3: <u>Tor</u> Adversary Goals & Attacks

If you were working for the KGB in the 1950s, one of your prime directives as an agent would be to gather as much intel on your enemy as possible, and work via methods of subversion as well as employ every other tool at your disposal to learn why your enemy does what he does. You would monitor his movements, correlate intel with other agents so as to promote predictability, and try to outmaneuver any mounting defenses with regards to their own intel gathering. Tor is not so different in this regard, but thankfully exploits and bugs are found and patched with impressive alacrity. It is not only the annoying gnats of internet society such as spammers, script kiddies and hackers that regularly try to poke holes in Tor's security blanket. Intelligence agencies (NSA), governments (China/Iran) and law enforcement do the same. They all have a common goal: find weaknesses in Tor's onion-routing mechanism and exploit it for their own goals. This includes circumventing the Tor button extension as well as many other addons for the Tor browser that can be added in with the free Tor application. Let's explore the goals of the Tor adversary first.

The most important goal is of course to bypass the proxy settings that is present in a Tor configuration. The aim here is to cause the user (or coerce) to make a more direct connection to a hostile IP address that the adversary has pre-chosen. It may happen that this cannot be done in as direct as fashion as the enemy wants. It is possible that the Tor user has configured the settings in such a way as to minimize the risk of such an occurrence. In that case, the next best thing is to settle for a correlation attack. That is, use a correlation method to identify something that the Tor user did outside of the Tor network and correlate it with something that occurred while he was using Tor. There are many methods of executing such an attack.

Cookies, javascript, fonts and elements of CSS code have all been used by adversaries as a means of identifying Tor users, along with a host of other exploitable browser elements at their disposal.

Cookies: A cookie may seem quite harmless to someone new to Tor. However in the vicinity of the Tor network, you want to take precautions against attacks on your anonymity. Never use the same browser that you do for the Tor network that you do for your non-Tor activities. Flash-based cookies can be coded in such a way as to correlate your Tor actions with your non-Tor actions to discover your IP address. Further, don't visit the same forums you do outside of Tor unless you're absolutely certain that no one can do any kind of language analysis on your comments and deduce you are the same person on Tor as outside of Tor. Familiarity not only breeds contempt, it breeds overconfidence.

Javascript: For the uninitiated Tor user, this one element of a browser can completely undermine one's anonymity on the Tor network. Not disabling this in the browser options can result in event handlers and timers being executed. This could be used to expose the true IP address, as the browser history function can be utilized to discover visited links via search engines, websites and social media addons. The timezone function can also be vulnerable when javascript queries it, in addition to revealing the operating system and type of cpu. Ultimately, what may not immediately reveal your IP address will certainly narrow the scope on your true location.

Fonts: Flash and Java plugins provide an enormous amount of data on the browser in question, so much so that it is possible to build an evolving profile on the user. What this means is that you can be "fingerprinted" more easily than you think. Therefore, do not use system fonts (i.e. your system) in your browser, but rather only those that come with your Tor bundle. It is better that everyone on the Tor network strive to use the same fonts (i.e. a global set). Many Tor beginners will completely ignore this advice and use the same browser for both Tor and non-Tor uses and ignore the disabling of plugins. They may scoff at having two browsers with completely separate bookmarks and settings, but as the adage says, luck favors the prepared. Having dozens of different functioning plugins complicates the effort to remain anonymous. Keeping things simple (uncluttered) is a better companion to anonymity than complexity, as the inner workings of most plugins are not well-known by most users who add them into the Tor browser.

Dynamic CSS: Css can be used to query fonts (i.e. font enumeration) per the explanation above. They can also implement CSS pop-ups, which are event handlers that can retrieve data from the CSS "mouse-over" attribute. Loading them in different Tor states can undermine anonymity, even if javascript is turned off. Again, be mindful of adding unique fonts that few users employ in their Tor sessions.

Exit Nodes: An adversary with sufficient resources at their disposal can run exit nodes and can sniff traffic that exits such nodes. This is a bit out of your hands at the moment, but it may be worthwhile to consider offering your bandwidth as a node as well. There are perks to this that are described on the Tor website.

Old Builds: It might be that a Tor user prefers to use an older browser on a not-too-common operating system. This too can be used to narrow down the field of selection and undermine anonymity. It is important to keep everything related to a Tor session as up-to-date as possible as to minimize risk of unfixed exploits.

Adservers: Someone can easily use an adserver to inject malicious code into a flash-based ad, which can anonymously send your IP address through the Tor network to the recipient. Outside of Tor, adservers are notorious for doing this as it provides more laser-targeted ads that drive up profits, but at the loss of your privacy and security.

Multi-Browser Attributes: Contrary to common opinion, an increasingly large number of browser attributes that are exploitable make anonymity more difficult to maintain over a long period of time. If enough data can be obtained about a particular user's browser, it can weaken anonymity. The browser window resolution, along with titlebar font and size, desktop resolution and browser plugins can severely impact one's anonymity. If you are one to pack your browser to the gills with plugins of every size, shape and color, identifying your non-Tor session with your Tor session will not be as difficult as you think.

Keyloggers: Perhaps more a threat than even Javascript, the damage imposed by these menaces of malware can completely defeat Tor and everything outside it. Usually, keyloggers are not a threat by visiting websites alone. They must be downloaded and executed on the host machine, either by you (by accident) or someone else (a cafe). Usually they will reside hidden inside an .exe file and once unleashed, might install itself as a service on the machine, recording every keystroke made. This not only defeats Tor, but also all encryption that accompanies a passphrase. The passphrase, along with all subsequent keystrokes, are sent to a recipient over the network it was installed on. I have found some anti-virus applications better suited for detection (SpyDoctor) and others (Norton) not so much. There are also free applications such as SpyBot which should be scheduled for daily scanning.

Nics: The use of forums to communicate have exploded over the last decade. Many security experts have advised against using the same passwords on multiple forums. The same should be same of nicknames. If you use the username "SarahParker382" on one forum outside of Tor, you will leave a footprint if you use it on a Tor forum since doing this makes it unlikely that the non-Tor user is someone else. Use common names like John, Mary, Jane, etc to minimize targeting and maximize anonymity. Names of movies and books also help, but do not add the same numbers to them that you do outside Tor.

Language Use: When you use region-specific spellings like "labour", "colour" and the like, you narrow the field of vision to your host country (i.e. UK, Canada or Australia). Avoid these kinds of terms if you are discussing sensitive information with another in a country hostile to free speech.

Search Engines: Be very cautious about visiting search engines via Tor, such as those that are connected to Google, Yahoo and Bing. You should ideally block all google services such as google-analytics or any other kinds of marketing services if at all possible. Even if cookies are disabled, Google can fingerprint your profile and make anonymity difficult. If you absolutely must use a search engine while using Tor, use one that you would not normally use outside of Tor (i.e. NOT Google, Bing, or Yahoo). The idea here is to build a profile for yourself that is 100% different than your non-Tor profile, right down to the language you use to communicate. This also goes for search queries that you manually input into search websites. Remember that Google records all searches related to local geographical location (restaurants, schools, government buildings, Google Maps/Google Earth).

Email: You would be surprised at how many Tor users actually use their real email address to communicate via Tor. If you have even connected to your email even once outside of Tor, that email should not be used for anything via Tor, since your IP address has most certainly been recorded by the email host, and can be subpoenaed by a judge.

Alcohol/Drugs: Like operating machinery, it seems some think that a bottle of scotch is of no consequence in using Tor. However remember that under the influence, you're more prone to reveal more about yourself than you would if you were sober. This is true in your favorite bar, and it is true online. Keep this in mind when you're visiting a forum and someone asks you to fire up a Skype session to chat with them, or asks anything related to your name, residence, favorite foods, etc.

Username/Password Forums on Tor: Inputing any kind of identity on Tor narrows the focus of any investigation, and this includes using usernames and passwords. You wouldn't think of logging into Facebook or Twitter on Tor, so why do it with any other forum? Doing so chips away anonymity.

"This persistence as private firms continued because it ensured the maximum of anonymity and secrecy to persons of tremendous public power who dreaded public knowledge of their activities as an evil almost as great as inflation."
- Carroll Quigley

Chapter 4: SHA1 values

For those of you who like to share music on networks such as Limewire, Emule, Bearshare and the like, you might wonder how it is that people get busted and/or sued by the record industry in doing so. It really doesn't take much to tell if a copyrighted song is being offered in a share folder at all. The company doesn't need to download and listen to the mp3 to check if it is really the music artist in question. They don't even need to look at the file name. What happens is this: an algorithm or program connects with your IP address while you are on the p2p network, then attempts to download the file that you are either in the process of downloading or seeding, and checks the hash value (md5 of SHA-1 hash, or Secure, Hash Algorithm) and verifies the 40 character value string against a database of recent albums released by the company. If the hash value matches, then it's a green light to send a nasty letter to the ISP from which the IP address was derived. From there, all manner of lawsuits can initiate, suing people for millions of dollars for only sharing a handful of songs. Since it is impossible that two sets of data would have the exact same hash and not be the same file, the powers that be feel that mistakes in identity are simply not possible, at least as it applies to data sets. If I wanted to send someone a word document, and he wanted to verify that it was actually the one I sent, all he would have to do is match the hash of the document with the hash of the original before I sent it to determine if it had been tampered with. Further, it doesn't take sharing a thousand different files on a public p2p network to attract attention. There have been many cases where someone was sued for millions on account of a couple dozen songs worth of music being available on Limewire and the Gnutella network.

Law enforcement works in a similar fashion. They have their own toolkit created by a Wyoming FBI agent that also checks file hashes on p2p networks. In this case, they check the hash being seeded and compare it to a database of hashes derived from known porn videos. If they get enough matches, then a law enforcement agent will investigate further, even executing a netstat command and/or examining the complete list of files the user is sharing. Then they get a subpoena for subscriber information from their ISP, find their address, and execute a swat-style raid at 6am to throw them off guard and confiscate any contraband. This of course assumes their pc is powered on, and most of the time they will know if there is network activity since they will have been monitoring the suspect for some time in a much more intimate fashion than sitting in a government cubicle a thousand miles away.

Needless to say, they need to know the *true* IP address of the user in question for this strategy to work. This works on every single p2p network and can even work on torrent users, since they too expose the IP address on the systems they utilize. When the true IP address is hidden, then all bets are off. Unfortunately for users of Tor, I2P, and Freenet , obscuring or hiding one's identity has attracted every type of online misfit you can think of: spammers, identity thieves, counterfeiters (both in money and in software), drug dealers, hired assassins and fraudsters. This is the price of true freedom and thus, anonymity. Though the good often has outweighed the bad, there have been those that have sought to blur the true purpose of anonymity and privacy.

In Louisiana (State v. Daigle, 2012), a Gnutella user who was arrested for the possession of illegal porn, argued that although a previous case (US v. Stults, 2009) had established that a person should not expect to be protected by the shield of privacy laws regarding the exposure of shared online files (i.e. mp3s, videos, etc), the very existence of the SHA identities themselves dictated a breach of privacy law where his prosecution was concerned. Perhaps he was equating the SHA values with a human's DNA (i.e. personhood).

"Defendant next claims that he had an expectation of privacy in the SHA values for his files as SHA means Secure Hash Algorithm. By its very name, it implies an expectation of privacy. Moreover, Defendant had an expectation of privacy because his files were encrypted and firewall-protected. Defendant equates Detective Gremillion's viewing the SHA values for his files to a law enforcement officer climbing a fence to look inside someone's window."

The problem with this line of reasoning is that it contradicts the privacy law he is attempting to cite in favor for his case. The SHA values are in no way equivalent to someone's DNA strand (i.e. a police officer looking over the fence at someone). Further, the very fact that he left them in the shared folder in the first place is indicative of him knowing that said files were in full view of the public, similar to what one would witness on a fruit stand on the side of the road. All the fruits are available for anyone passing by.   If the fruit stand owners really wanted privacy, they would have sold/traded their fruit behind closed doors and not marketed them to the open public, or in this case of the defendant, on an open p2p network with his IP address exposed for weeks/months on end. Therefore, the IP address is the digital map that leads to your very doorstep. That is how he was busted. It is not the first time however that someone ignorantly confused privacy with anonymity. Sarah Palin's email hacker had erroneously concluded that an IP address was of no consequence. He didn't use Tor, or any other public or private proxy to hide his tracks, and was summarily arrested not long after he accessed her Yahoo email account. The Yahoo email header from a screenshot gave his identity away. With the header visible, FBI agents, with Yahoo's assistance, were able to pinpoint his location. If he had used Tor, he would have gotten away clean.

Using the hacker example, if the perpetrator in question had used full-disk encryption, it would have made the prosecution of said individual infinitely more troublesome to execute. Why? Because the network footprints that would have sealed his fate before a jury would have most likely resided on his C: drive (i.e. boot drive), as well as the SHA-1 values of *any* type of file, be they videos, pictures or love letters. Now, the court could certainly have tried to coerce him into forking over the pass phrase if it was Truecrypt protected, however this would have violated his Fifth Amendment right against self-incrimination. If some court was able to get the pass phrase from him, it would have done them no good if he had use the "hidden partition" option that Truecrypt offers, which as we have described, offers two passwords: one for the decoy container or operating system, and one for the real container or operating system.

You might wonder what kinds of things they can use against you if they have access to your boot drive. Worry more about what kinds of things a criminal can do. Law enforcement agents are restrained from prosecuting you if it is illegal to do so. They are bound by the courts, and the law. Criminals on the other hand have no such restrictions. Identity thieves have ways of looking through your browsing history to find passwords, credit card numbers, email usernames and access passwords, and other financial transcriptions. Having a fully-encrypted boot disk ensures that if you are away from your house and your computer is stolen, the thieves responsible cannot use said computer to obtain email usernames and access passwords, and other financial information. Having a fully-encrypted boot disk ensures that if you are away from your house and your computer is stolen, the thieves responsible cannot use anything on the root C: hard drive, as it would be nothing but encrypted information. It is much easier to deal with a loss of a $500-$800 computer versus thousands of dollars in defrauded credit card purchases and illegal bank account withdrawals.

In any event, remember that the IP address is not shared with anyone else while you are using. Thus, it has a trail of timestamps littered across the internet. And a SHA value is likewise not shared by any other file. If you are ever sued and a court orders the police to confiscate your computer, unless it is encrypted, everything you have done online will be viewable by anyone, regardless of what files you have manually deleted from the hard drive. Only a free space wipe of the drive will secure deleted files (i.e. CCleaner).

"Well, I don't think I've ever consciously come up with tricks and tools to, kind of, hide. I do think I'm a bit more vigilant, in terms of safety issues and things. And sometimes it is kind of nice to try to hold onto your anonymity."
- Calista Flockhart

Chapter 5: Securing Your Hard Drive of Sensitive Documents

Online anonymity in and of itself has become easier to understand and implement over the last decade, so much so that anyone who knows how to install an operating system can eradicate their online shadow by installing just a few programs and adhering to a few common sense rules. The same can certainly be said of encryption. Unfortunately, a myth still perpetuates itself that one needs a master's degree in computer science in order to encrypt their hard drive. You would be surprised how many think along these lines, and how many have had their lives destroyed by a prosecutor with open access to said hard drive. So let's clear up some misconceptions that exist, at least in the West, where the idea has flourished that you need to be a computer geek to use full disk encryption and it's just "too hard" for the average Joe off the street.

Before we jump into the subject of encrypting one's disk, it should be said that you should not fall into the mindset that you will be able to eradicate all traces of your online activity from your hard drive completely. There will always be fragmented thumbnails, registry entries, shortcuts and of course the ever present deleted files that still linger about between the deleted spaces. If you really feel like you absolutely have to take some kind of precautions in the event your computer is stolen, then use CCleaner (free). While it does do a competent job of cleaning house, so to speak, it is the "wipe free space" function that is perhaps the most valuable, and one that is sorely lacking with most on-the-fly encryption programs. It is amazing that, even post-2012, most computer users think that when you delete a file, that it is permanently gone once you empty the recycle bin. All the recycle bin does is tell the hard drive that the space once occupied by said file can be written to again. Nothing has really been erased unless that particular space has been copied over again with new data. On the subject of deleted files, it is ridiculously simple for even an amateur Pc or Mac user to use off-the-shelf recovery software to retrieve said files if the space has not been overwritten to. If it is easy for an amateur user, imagine the tools an experienced forensics investigator has at their disposal. With that said, what then is the solution for all of these fragmented files laying about the drive? The solution is full-disk encryption.

Full Disk Encryption (Skip this section if you already have Truecrypt)
Even if you skip the plausible deniability option of Truecrypt (installing hidden partition option), you will still have the ability to lock out forensic investigators, government agencies, corrupt agents of the State, and anyone else who wishes to pry into your affairs. With Truecrypt (free), you can set the option to have a password request at system boot. Naturally, no password means the system doesn't boot. It also allows you to create locked containers, where upon entry of the password, "unlocks" the container and loads the image as if it were an external hard drive of SD card plugged into the pc. Don't worry, Truecrypt will tell you if it can't perform the install.

Setting up a basic configuration of Truecrypt is ridiculously simple.

I. Download Truecrypt (free) at http://www.truecrypt.org/downloads. Make sure you choose the correct version for your own operating system
II. Run the setup file that you downloaded, then check "Agree" to the license.
III. After choosing Accept, choose Next when done, and you'll see the option to install to a directory of your choice.

After installation you can create Hidden Truecrypt volumes by choosing "create volume" from the Truecrypt menu. Select "create an encrypted file container" and select next. Then select "hidden Truecrypt volume", Normal Mode, and then on "Select File". Next, choose a file name with a Truecrypt extension, such as sample.tc. It doesn't matter where, and you can choose any filename you like. Just make sure you note the Truecrypt extension (i.e. .tc), otherwise you will have to use the Truecrypt interface to browse for and unlock/decrypt the container.
Note: It doesn't matter where you put this file on your computer. If your hard drive is ever confiscated for whatever reason, any competent forensics investigator will find it no matter where you store it. What they will not find, however, is your passphrase to open said container, provided you have not written it down (a bad habit to get into).
After typing a filename and using explorer to browse to a save location, click Save, and make sure "Never save history is checked". On the "Outer Volume" display, choose the default hash as it's suitable for your needs, then choose a file size. I would recommend at least ten gigabytes if you can spare it. It will ask you for a password. Choose a password that is suitably long, say thirty characters. Most people cannot remember that many,

however you can use an eight character password and then repeat it several times, provided it is NOT a password you have ever used before, which includes bank sites, educational sites or forums. These too can be subpoenaed by a judge in an attempt to obtain passwords for the forensics team.

Truecrypt will ask you to create two passwords, one for the outer volume (where the decoy info will be dumped) and one for the inner volume (where your sensitive info will be dumped, such as love letters, credit card info, security intel, classfied info, etc). These two encrypted passwords will be used for the SAME Truecrypt container.

Now, you might be wondering at this point, why use two passwords and not just one? Well, you can certainly use ONE password for a Truecrypt volume. However, laws in the UK can be used against you to fork over the password for a volume that doesn't have a hidden container. What we are doing essentially is creating a treasure chest inside another treasure chest, only when the French Armada opens the chest with the outer password, they see emptiness. They do not even know that an invisible treasure chest sits within it. If a UK judge issues an order by the court to compel you to give the password for the outer volume, you can rest assured of your safety and hand it over to them in the confidence that they cannot technically know if a hidden compartment even exists.

Best Practices:
I. Do not store anything incriminating in the outer container. Additionally, do not enclose anything that would be seen as an attack on the State (i.e. Iran, China, etc).
II. Be aware that using financial statements, academic transcripts, love letters, immigration papers and credit card

information may fall into the wrong hands if you deposit any of these in the wrong volume.

III. Once you have finished dumping the decoy files inside, never add any further files to the OUTER container (the INNER container is fine however for adding files), as you can damage the inner volume's contents by doing so.

IV. Never under any circumstances leave your laptop or pc powered ON when you are not in front of it. If someone is able to install any kind of keylogger, then Truecrypt (and everything else) is defeated. Permanently. You will be entering your passwords as the keylogger records every stroke you make upon the keyboard, and will silently send them online to some unknown, nefarious entity up to no good. Needless to say, this happens mostly in public places like cafes, airports and the like, where identity thieves lurk in waiting for unsuspecting but naive users to leave their laptop unattended for a brief restroom break.

There, all done. It only seems complicated because you have never done it before. Anything worth doing usually has a learning curve in the beginning, and the benefits of using Truecrypt far outweigh the temporary uncomfortable half-hour that you must spend on learning about its abilities. It can potentially save you years of tortuous financial difficulties, as well as perhaps saving your life someday.

"With false names, on the right nets, they could be anybody. Old men, middle-aged women, anybody, as long as they were careful about the way they wrote. All that anyone would see were the words, their ideas. Every citizen started equal, on the nets."
— Orson Scott Card, Enders Game

Chapter 6: Don't Talk to Cops

In 2010, one particular video went viral on YouTube and a few other miscellaneous video sites. There is nothing unusual about that, since thousands go viral every day. However this particular video, called "Don't Talk to Cops", let the general public in on most of the basic as well as advanced tactics law enforcement uses in their forensic studies and discussions with suspects. At the heart of it was the Fifth Amendment guaranteed by the US Constitution, which stated you have the right against self-incrimination. However what the public wasn't aware of was the depth of guile and deceit law enforcement officers use to get around this right. Encryption is at the heart of the video since by law you cannot be compelled to be a witness against yourself by giving away the password. The video is an absolute must-see if you are not very knowledgeable about what the police force can do and what they cannot do.

It may happen that someone uses your over-the-air wi-fi connection without asking. It could be someone parked down the street from you. Perhaps they are using it to secure payment for an illegal drug ring, or they could be issuing death threats via email to their place of employment and need to hide their IP address to do so, or perhaps they want to hack into a government database. Whatever the case may be, you can be sure of two things. The first is that they want to conceal their IP address and use yours to commit the crime. And two, it is you who will get blamed for it, not them.

If you are arrested for any kind of online activity in the United States, the best thing to do is to vocally administer your right to remain silent. As of June, 2010, the Supreme Court has ruled that you must now vocally invoke the right to remain silent. Staying silent in and of itself will not ward off the police interrogation (also known as the "Interview").

http://voices.washingtonpost.com/supreme-court/2010/06/supreme_court_rules_in_miranda.html

You are under no obligation at all to talk to any kind of law enforcement concerning your online activities (or offline for that matter). In some cases, they will do what is called a "knock and talk", where they will physically visit your address and after knocking on your door, attempt to talk you into admitting something that didn't actually happen. The entire ordeal is based on deception, a tactic the CIA is intimately familiar with. When they cite your Miranda rights: "anything you say can and will be used against you", what they arc essentially saying is this: "we're going to interrogate you and try to convince you that giving us every detail we ask for will benefit you in some fashion". However, nothing could be further from the truth. Every word out of your mouth from the moment any law enforcement agent approaches you can be used against you, and most certainly it will if you are arrested. The police are not your friend. That is not their job. Their job is to provide enough evidence to the prosecutor to build a case against you that will stand up to scrutiny in court. In a majority of cases, the defendant gives them all the rope they need for a public hanging in front of a jury simply because they did not keep their mouth shut and ask for an attorney. Innocent people have gone to prison, sometimes for decades, because they erroneously assumed that talking to the police was in their best interests. It clearly was not. The police are also allowed by law to lie to you, just as the CIA is. You however, can be charged for lying to the police. The solution? Say nothing, since even if you tell nothing but the truth, you can still be framed for a crime if they have no one else to pin it on. This actually happens far more frequently than you have been led to believe. When/if you are brought in, they will try and get you to talk in what they call an "interview". It is an interrogation designed to trick you into self-incrimination. Ask for a lawyer and say you wish to invoke your Fifth Amendment right against self-incrimination. Nothing else. In any case, they are not in any position whatsoever to offer a plea deal (though they will attempt to convince you otherwise). Plea deals come from the prosecution, not the police force. The moment you open your mouth should be only in the presence of your attorney.

You may think that law enforcement has never assisted in any case involving the sharing of online files, and that the prosecution has only been fixated upon those sharing mp3 files. You would be mistaken, since the court cannot enforce anything on their own without the assistance of the police. That is the symbiotic relationship between them and the courts. They depend upon one another for their existence. There have been cases where internet users have not secured their Wi-Fi connection, and thus have left their connection open to other law-breaking citizens. There was a case in Milford, Massachusetts in 2010 that involved a family with an unsecured Wi-Fi connection. Someone had used their connection to obtain illicit pornography files online. The end result? Their house was raided by FBI agents in the early dawn hours. Not only were they emotionally abused by the agents, they were lied to and treated like terrorists. In addition, their computers were confiscated and not returned for two years. During this time, they were not told any details on the status of said computers by either the FBI or anyone connected to the federal government. Corrupt? You be the judge.

There have been many law enforcement types (detectives, cops, even captains) who have stated time and time again that a majority of their cases have been solved and/or led to an arrest without the need for a warrant. This is due primarily to the way law enforcement approaches suspects. They will typically try and engage the suspect or suspect's friends or family in a "friendly chat" to smooth things over and sort out any difficulties. The only thing "smoothed out" by talking to a police officer or detective without consulting an attorney first is going to be a warrant for your arrest. It is not enough to say that "anything can be used against you". That much is certainly true. However what the adage should say is, "everything will be used against you". Certainly nothing you say will help your case at all. Think carefully before you say a word.

There are some very stark differences between the US and the UK. In the UK, if you don't give your Truecrypt (or Drivecrypt, PGP, etc) password to the court, you can be imprisoned for up to two years on a contempt of court charge. This is much harder to do in the US. If you have "claimed ownership" of the files inside an encrypted volume publicly to any law enforcement agent, you too can be charged with contempt for not divulging your password to the judge. This is why having TWO passwords on any Truecrypt container or encrypted operating system is paramount. One for the outer volume, and one for the inner volume.

"A desire for privacy does not imply shameful secrets; Moglen argues, again and again, that without anonymity in discourse, free speech is impossible, and hence also democracy. The right to speak the truth to power does not shield the speaker from the consequences of doing so; only comparable power or anonymity can do that."
- Nick Harkaway, *The Blind Giant*

Chapter 7: The Weakest Link: Human Fallibility & Ego

I once went hiking in the Appalachian mountains, and while I had an amateurish level of experience in regards to surviving in the great outdoors, it always struck me as odd that some of my fellow hikers seemed to always over-prepare for what was essentially a four hour walk in the woods. I would discover later that you can never take too many precautions when dealing with Mother Nature. The unpredictability of the elements, as well as predators such as grizzlies, wolves and snakes can certainly negate any perceived over preparedness. In short, my ego would be my undoing. After getting lost for two days, which is admittedly child's play next to what some unprepared hikers experience, Nature taught me some valuable lessons regarding my flawed dependence on technology and how much more important it was to depend on the signs of mother nature rather than solely relying on my GPS device.

Trails can be a great thing when you're lost. Quite often in out of the way places such as forests, deserts and the like, we can better find our way to civilization by treading the well worn path before us. Likewise, traveling the road less taken certainly has its natural charm; it is our overconfidence that propels us toward danger. There exists a touch of irony to how we traverse unworn trails online. People love the familiar. Facebook, Twitter, LinkedIn and Google lull them into a false sense of security, similar to what a fisherman sees as he glances down into the water. A handful of fish dart around the bait, some hesitating out of a sense of danger and deception, until one fish finally grabs the hook, and at which point the true identity is revealed. Social Media is similar in that people feel secure around lists of friends, relatives, and co-workers that share the same politics, movie stars and war heroes.

Establishing Trails: When I drive to Tim Horton's to buy an ice cappuccino, I establish a physical as well as financial trail. There are all manner of recording devices that dash any hopes of anonymity: my license plate/color & make of my car, my debit card used, and security cams on the way to the location. Likewise when I am online, and making a purchase, I leave an even bigger trail, since now multiple ad entities like Google, Facebook and the like can track every click I make provided they have installed the right cookie on my machine.

Overconfidence & the Ego: If I fire up the Tor network and start my browsing session without disabling javascript, or use the same browser on the Tor network that I use for my non-Tor sessions, then I have left a clear trail to my real identity on Tor. This can be a result of switching from a fast-performing service like Usenet or BitTorrent and then immediately jumping onto the Tor network which can be intermittently slow. Tor is a completely different mindset than other systems.

Time and Familiarity Chip Away at Caution and Experience: The more we use something, or for that matter, do something, the more likely it is that our confidence with our skillset will cement in our subconscious, so much so that we grow over-confident. You must not allow this to happen. Sometimes it happens to base jumpers with years of experience. They get cocky, and start taking unnecessary risks. Sure enough, Nature often corrects the anomaly with frightening results. It is easy to get lulled in a sense of absolute security if you use Tor on a daily basis. Be on guard however for those times when you have the same bookmarks and accidentally login to the same forum with the same username and password (i.e. alcohol & Tor do not mix!).

Javascript Links: When you first fire up Tor, you may not notice that the Tor devs decided it would be a great idea to have javascript enabled automatically since, as they put it, "some websites won't work without it". Your first priority should be to disable this in the browser options at your first opportunity. How careless would it be for a first time base jumper to not check his reserve parachute's security? Likewise, you should not put blind faith in Tor developers without first testing it yourself to see if all the kinks and hole have been ironed out or patched.

Foreign Identities: During the war in Iraq, there was once a sign that was secured above the mess hall that said, "Be polite. Be civil, but have a plan to kill anyone you meet". Many chat rooms work well with Tor in addition to Freenet, I2P and other systems. However as a security precaution you should always assume, even in the smallest recess of your mind, that the person you are talking to might not be all they claim to be. They could be an adversarial attorney, a law enforcement officer, a tax evasion investigator, your wife, etc. In short, don't let slip any details of your personal life in a private chat room that you wouldn't air out in a public forum on Tor. Trust, but verify.

"Sacrificing anonymity may be the next generation's price for keeping precious liberty, as prior generations paid in blood."
— Hal Norby

Chapter 8: Social Media and the Anti-Anonymity Engines

As previously mentioned, those that design the engines of social media and search engines know that anonymous tools like Tor, Freenet, I2P, and others do not lend themselves well to targeted advertising. Using any of the above programs make it impossible for them to gather data on its users: which movies they prefer, which movies to suggest, and which movie stars latest divorce is making the headlines. So to solve this dilemma they make it frustrating for Tor users, for example, to use its search engine. They will frequently give errors or require captchas in order to use their search tools. Facebook does the same with those who use Tor to try to login to their accounts, giving them warnings that state they are suspicious of their location login from say, Germany as opposed to the usual login location of Dallas, Texas. All of this is due to the fact they can tell when a person is using Tor, but not where they're true geo-location is. Thus, any pay-per-click ad that is shown is a fairly wasted campaign since most Tor users are on the Tor network to enhance anonymity, not eliminate it by whipping out their credit card to buy something PPC related.

Purpose of Search Engines: 1996 vs. 2012

Back before Google became a corporate behemoth, there were a few search engines that had one aim: provide the user with what he was searching for. These included AltaVista, Infoseek, Yahoo and a host of others. Millions of students across North America didn't have to worry about every private detail of their lives being exchanged and bartered behind their backs from the likes of LinkedIn, Twitter, and Google. Fast forward to 2012. Now, just about every search engine you can think of makes their money not only from ads, but by building profiles based on your browsing history. Don't have a Google Plus account? Not to worry. If you are surfing out in the open, Google probably has enough data on your habits to build a ghost profile for you without your consent, and it just may happen that the day you sign up, they have already amassed a wealth of information concerning where you work as well as who your co-workers and family members are. The Facebook tag system is notoriously anti-privacy in this regard, with the algorithm being able to correlate names with face recognition technology. Needless to say, you should never entertain the idea of posting pictures of yourself, your friends or your family on any Tor website, Freesite or blog.

Making Anonymity Obsolete

The "enhancement" of being able to recognize what your family members and friends are thinking or doing 24/7 has been an effective tool in duping the masses into believing that they simply can't live without social media as an integral part of their lives. The word "integral" is grossly misused by both the media and users the world over. There are many billions of people who live comfortable lives in the world without Facebook, for example. They get all of the benefits of a face-to-face relationship with none of the drawbacks of a social media network. It certainly could be argued that identity theft is a problem for the digital masses; however it is the current mechanisms of social media that are eroding one's personal identity more than slick thieves who hack away code in cellars a half-world away. Thieves will steal only what they think they can get away with in the here and now. Behemoths like Facebook and Google will not only alter your identity to better fit their projections slowly over a long period of time, they will make you feel as if you had willingly given them this power, or as they say, "opted-in". The Terms of Service for both Facebook and Google change as frequently as the wind changes directions. Most users simply click "Next" whenever they have to sign something as quickly as they can. They almost never read the fine print. Likewise, most eighteen-year old students sign on the dotted line for student loans, regardless of major, and rarely plot out a financial plan of gauging just how much interest they will have to pay back. They just want to get out of their parents house and go where their herd of friends are going. Facebook is no different, and likewise has a high price to pay in the long run.

The most egregious element of all of these anti-anonymity services is that they are exceedingly hypocritical in sharing a user's personal information with everyone else. The username and pass feature shared by multiple services is a slap in the face of every security precautionary measure in the world. Facebook for instance wants you to give them your passwords to other services, but doesn't want to allow them to login. It is not only putting all of your nest eggs in one basket: it is putting them all within striking distance of a den of foxes. When you first invest in the stock market, your manager likely will tell you to diversify your stocks, yet Facebook and Google will tell you it is better to trust all the Big Brands of the Internet for your own good. Nothing could be further from the truth, as they stand to benefit the most, and you stand to lose the most. When no social media network can trace your online footprint, then they consider you a threat to them simply because spammers may have used a similar anonymous means to cause mischief. It is akin to a teacher punishing the entire class because one student cheated on a test.

Faulty Designs and Keeping it SIMPLE:
It seems axiomatic in a sense that when companies become big enough, they start the "one-step-forward, two-steps back" routine of sub-optimization. They will exceed their customer's wishes for a few years to the point where they feel they can't live without their product. Then when their brand is world renown, they will try even harder to reach the billion-per-year profit margins, only to fall flat on its face. Microsoft did this with Windows Vista. Facebook's interface and privacy policy settings are now a confusing mess compared to the simple panorama they once were. Google's motto was once "Do No Evil", yet now they are the bane of the end user, spamming most of their front page with PPC ads instead of the relevant content the user was searching for in the first place. LinkedIn is now trying to hook up its members to every social media fountain on the planet.

Tor on the other hand has actually gotten simpler to use, as has Freenet. Both represent a threat model to the aforementioned brands because they give tremendous influence and power back to the *individual.* Through your own research you will find Google and the like to have actually donated some of their profits to the creators of these anonymous tools. Remember that Google donates for all kinds of unique and creative open-source projects, including outer space projects. They like to keep tabs on the development process, as well as offering "advice" to the developers (whether the devs accept the advice is another matter entirely). If you know your enemy's defenses inside and out, you can better develop a more strategic offensive to counteract its anonymous efficiency. Thankfully Google is no closer to cracking Tor or Freenet than they were years ago. However, the adage "Know Thy Enemy" is their modus operandi.

"Who are you?"
"No one of consequence."
"I must know."
"Get used to disappointment."
- William Goldman, *The Princess Bride*

Chapter 9: Freenet Best Practices

I touched on the basics of using Freenet in my first book, Darknet: How to Stay Anonymous Online, but avoided going into too much depth regarding correlation attacks and weaknesses of the system for purposes of simplification. Put bluntly, Freenet needs more users. The system runs faster and generally more efficiently with a larger amount of users donating ever bigger datastores for the network. The datastore is created by you, on your hard drive. It can be one gigabyte in size or one hundred. The higher the datastore, the better Freenet runs. Unfortunately, a bit of patience is required to get the most out of Freenet.

If you have never heard of Freenet, there is probably a good reason for it. It is not as simple to use as say, Facebook, Twitter or MySpace. You probably will not find any of your relatives or friends on it unless you purposely invite them and establish a Darknet link exchanging node references with each other. It has been my experience that Freenet actually offers a level of anonymity that is a few levels stronger than Tor, but there are of course some serious drawbacks. First, it cannot connect to the normal web. You won't be able to connect to Facebook, or any social media site for that matter. You will however be able to connect to Freesites, their darknet equivalent, by typing in its Freenet address into your browser. Secondly, unlike Tor, your IP address is out there for the whole world to see for the length of time that you're on the Freenet network. Unlike Tor, this is not a problem however, since the datastores themselves are encrypted end-to-end, and no one knows who requested which file, where it came from, or where it is going (unlike P2P networks). Third, it is brutally slow for the first 24-48 hours. So much so, that you may think nothing is going on under the hood. When I initially researched Freenet years ago, my gut was telling me that the engine was running but I wasn't going anywhere. You must not let this dissuade you from using it. Patience will get you far in this network.

The Basics in a Nutshell

You can download Freenet at https://freenetproject.org/

It is highly advised to let Freenet run for 24 hours in order to find random nodes to connect to. Don't expect to get Torrent-like speeds with Freenet. It is not built for speed, but rather for keeping the data and messages you send through its digital conduits anonymous.

Freenet Vulnerabilities

Unlike most other P2P systems, it actually matters what you say on Freenet boards. Like Tor, you can quite easily give away your geographical location if you are not careful. Geographical spellings like "colour" and "labour" can reveal that you are either in the UK or Canada. This is mostly a problem only in conjunction with other leaks of personal information, such as a list of your favorite sports team or local restaurant.

Node Reference: If you give anyone your node reference, they can link your IP address with your nick and reveal your true identity. You should only reveal this to sources that you trust 100%, such as those on your friends list. If you let slip your node reference on a message board in Frost, it will be viewable by thousands of Freenet users across the globe, and there is absolutely no deleting it from the boards. There are no moderators or administrators on Freenet in the sense that they can remove inserts from the network. Needless to say, having this level of free speech has some drawbacks, in that spammers and trolls like to target the network.

System Time: Make certain that your system time in your BIOS for your motherboard is set correctly. It can be used to correlate an attack and reveal your Freenet identity if it is not. While this method might not stand up to jury scrutiny in the US, it would certainly be disastrous for a Chinese or Iranian dissident wanting to keep his identity secret. There are a multitude of places online where you can synchronize your system time. The default tray icon in windows is insufficient in this regard. Restart your pc, then hit "delete" to see what timestamp your system is really relaying to the world.

Unexpected Visits: There is a bit of a paradox in the Freenet user guides out in the wild. On the one hand, you are encouraged to leave Freenet running 24/7 for maximum performance. However, even choosing Freenet's most stringent security option can leave your system open for a forensics or government team if your pc is running. Therefore, you might explore the option of running Freenet from an encrypted Truecrypt container. However even then, do not have Freenet running unless you are in front of your pc. This of course assumes you have full-disk encryption across the board (i.e. you've encrypted not only your sensitive data with Truecrypt containers, but also your operating system). In hostile countries like Iran, China and the like, even running Freenet at all can get you into trouble, since Freenet offers a way for its citizens to get messages to the outside world anonymously regarding human rights abuses. Nothing stirs up a communist hornet nest quite like free speech, and Freenet excels in providing this ability for free to anyone with the patience to learn the intricacies of Freenet.

Disable Firewire Port in BIOS: Not necessarily related to Freenet, but a good practice to engage in. The firewire port has been used in the past to retrieve encryption keys and other miscellaneous items from encrypted setups. If you absolutely have to use firewire, do so from a computer without sensitive information (i.e. Freenet, Tor, etc).

Using VMware images: In the past, some Freenet users have utilized the operating system emulator called VMware to run Freenet. The VMware operating system (Windows XP/7 for instance) will be encrypted with Truecrypt or some other relevant encryption protection, and will essentially be an encrypted operating system inside another encrypted operating system. This seems to be overkill as the virtual OS can leak information via the swap file on the host operating system. The allure is that if you are a Chinese dissident using Freenet, and you are raided, you only have one singular file in which to "shred" via a hard drive or file shredder nuke program like DBAN. However, there is every reason to believe that 1.) you will not have time to initiate *any* kind of program should government agents storm your residence) and 2.) there will almost certainly be traces of your correspondence elsewhere on your host system and 3.) using full-disk encryption is likely to be sufficient for purposes of staying anonymous. If they manage to install a keylogger on your system (either remotely or if they have physical access to your machine), having two encrypted operating systems, even if one is a hidden decoy via Truecrypt's plausible deniability method, you are toast. The keylogger can be stored in your keyboard (hardware) or installed as a service which hides in windows services (svchost) and is difficult for most anti-virus programs to detect.

Also by Lance Henderson:

Darknet: A Beginner's Guide To Staying Anonymous

Usenet and the Future of Anonymity

Dating in a Social Media World

Social Media in an Anti-Christian World

Social Media in an Anti-social World

Printed in Great Britain
by Amazon.co.uk, Ltd.,
Marston Gate.